I0491832

The Seven Petro-Wolves

By Tahereh Amirzadeh

Tahereh Amirzadeh is an Iranian oil & gas professional living in France.

She holds a Master of Science in International Management with specialization track in Oil & Gas from University of Liverpool Management School (ULMS), an Executive Advanced Master ("Mastère spécialisé") in Strategy & Management of International Business (SMIB) from ESSEC Business School and an Executive Advanced Master ("Mastère spécialisé") in Leading International Industrial Projects (LIIP) from École Polytechnique (L'X) and ESSEC Business School. She also has the following professional certifications: Liquefied Natural Gas (LNG) from IFP Training (IFP School); Combating Money Laundering and the Financing of Terrorism & Proliferation (AML/CFT) in Banks; Industry 4.0 from Technical University of Munich (TUM) School of Management; Professional Scrum Product Owner™ I (PSPO I) from Scrum.org; and, Lean Six Sigma Green Belt from a Training Associate (Lean Six Sigma Master Black Belt) accredited by International Association for Six Sigma Certification (IASSC).

Before joining the oil & gas industry, she was working in a private company specialized in trade finance and forfaiting worldwide, dealing with commercial insurance companies providing credit insurance and state-owned insurance companies – ECAs (Export Credit Agencies).

Summary

Foreword

Since its early days in the second half of the XIXth century, the world hydrocarbon industry has undergone major transformations, alongside more or less important changes which have progressively shaped the present landscape of the international oil and gas industries.

The overwhelming transformation has been by far the shift in the dominance of the world market from the large integrated companies, now known as the International Oil Companies (IOCs), or the "Seven Sisters", to the government-owned National Oil Companies (NOCs).

The key date of this shift has been the beginning of the 1970s, marked by the generalization of nationalizations and/or takeovers of reserves and assets of the former foreign oil concession companies by the oil and gas exporting countries in the Arab countries, following the first nationalizations decided in Mexico in 1938 and Iran in 1951 under Mohamed Mossadegh.

The most spectacular consequences of these nationalizations are illustrated by the fact that the IOCs that had fully controlled until then the world oil and gas markets, with the exclusive ownership of more than 90% of proven reserves and production, have suddenly lost this control to the benefit of NOCs, except less than 10% of oil and gas reserves and production they have retained in some countries. At the same time, the member nations of the Organization of Petroleum Exporting Countries (OPEC) decided to set themselves from now on the prices of their exports while increasing the same at the end of 1973 from around 2 to 7 dollars per barrel. The activities of foreign companies were simultaneously taken over by the new NOCs of the producing states. For these reasons, it can be considered that the said countries became actually real oil producing and exporting countries while before that period they were merely countries where foreign companies had the exclusivity and power to produce and export oil and set prices.

However, it is remarkable that the first national oil companies didn't come into existence in the aftermath of nationalizations in oil exporting countries but well before that in the main European industrialized countries eager to get rid of the dominant role of the mainly American IOCs in a sector as strategic as the import, refining and distribution of oil products. The pioneers in this regard have been, by chronological order, the United Kingdom where British Petroleum was created through a majority takeover of the former Anglo-Iranian Oil Company in 1914, France (Compagnie Française des Pétroles, CFP, in 1924), Italy (Agip in 1926 under Enrico Mattei), Mexico (Pemex, in 1938), Brazil (Petrobras, in 1953), Japan (Japex, in 1955) or India (ONGC, in 1956), followed by Germany (Deminex), Spain (Repsol) and other West European nations, without naturally forgetting China and the ex-USSR.

On the other hand, the large vacuum left by IOCs in the aftermath of nationalizations and takeovers as well as the lack of experience of NOCs during their first years of existence have prompted the setting up and rapid development of dozens of new service companies able to operate in all segments of the oil and gas activities. The largest are Halliburton, Baker Hughes, Schlumberger, Weatherford, Fluor, Black and Veach Pritchard, and Transocean. They sell their expertise and ever larger range of surface and subsurface services to NOCs as well as IOCs and independents.

For their part, and following the loss of their strongholds in major oil and gas producing nations, IOCs reoriented their strategies in two main directions, namely : 1) Recentering their activities on complex and costly plays and projects where their long experience gives them an undisputable comparative advantage, such as exploration in the Arctic and very deep seawater and presalt plays, as well as developing unconventional oil and gas resources, and, 2) Boosting their sharply reduced reserve assets through access to new ones, in the rare countries where this access is still possible, in the framework of associations with local NOCs, i.e. production sharing contracts (PSCs). This new form of contracts, which is now applied in more than 70 countries, gives actually IOCs and other foreign publicly traded companies the possibility to increase their own reserves and to book their share of discovered oil and gas, in conformity with the rules of the US Security and Exchange Commission.

Another less favorable option for IOCs is the contract service model, for which competition is becoming very tight with big service companies.

This rapid flyover of the hydrocarbon history remains uncomplete if it overlooks and doesn't take into consideration the human aspect, i.e. the crucial role played and the skills of some exceptional pioneers who started from nothing or with few means and succeeded in opening new ways and developing some major activities of the today's world oil and gas industries. The captivating itinerary of some of these pioneers, that one can call adventurers or visionaries is very well described, with many unknown and pleasant anecdotes, in the new book of Tahereh Amirzadeh under the title "The Seven Petro-Wolves".

The first of these wolves is John D. Rockefeller who was the first and real pioneer of the oil industry and more specifically the creator and father of what we call today multinational or international oil companies (IOCs). He started his oil business (late 1860s) in the United States in the oil exploration and production segment and he rapidly understood the necessity to control the entire supply chain from the upstream (exploration and production) to the downstream (retail outlets), going through midstream (storage and transportation). His business model was mainly based on economies of scale and control of the supply chain from A to Z and was the first example of vertical integration which was later adopted by other large oil and gas companies as well as in other large businesses.

This business model allowed Rockefeller to increase profits, to edge out competitors and to create an empire under the leadership of Standard Oil Company created in 1870 which, in 1879 controlled 90% of US refining capacity and most of the pipelines and distribution outlets in the United States.

By then Rockefeller became a legend and was considered as the richest man in the world.

Another oil wolf whose success story is very well explained in Tahereh Amirzadeh's book is William Knox D'Arcy. What is most surprising in the course of this British citizen is his determination to find oil in Persia where many other big investors had failed to do so, and in a region (Middle East) where nobody dared then to imagine the existence of huge oil and gas fields discovered some thirty years later.

The D'Arcy adventure started with a 60-year concession obtained in 1960 covering around three-quarters of the country. His only commitment was to pay the monarchy a mere 16% of any profits, without any review of his accounting.

Without any real business model, D'Arcy's dream was based on a kind of bet with rudimentary seismic and geological data, but without any reference to a discovery in this vast country. So it was not surprising that several exploration wells proved dry and put D'Arcy on the verge of bankruptcy. He was then obliged to accept the help and a participation of Burmah Oil Company, until oil was finally discovered in 1908. It was a major turning point in the oil history not only in Persia (now Iran) that became one of the leading world oil and gas countries but also in the Middle East where huge and many oil and gas fields were discovered between the first and the second world wars. During this period the center of gravity of the world oil and gas production has rapidly moved from the USA to Iran, Saudi Arabia, Iraq and other Gulf countries.

The original Anglo-Persian Oil Company became later Anglo-Iranian Oil Company and was nationalized in 1951 by Mossadegh government.

More recently, other so-called "oil wolves" comprise the Russian oligarch Mikhail Khodorkovsky, a former member of the USSR's Communist Party who has seized the occasion of the Perestroika and economic liberalization to create in 1987 with other partners the first private bank in the ex-USSR and to acquire later on assets developed formerly by the State. The biggest was Russia's second largest oil company, Yukos, purchased at a cost of no more than 309 million dollars. Two years later Yukos was listed on the stock market with a value of … 9 billion dollars, and Khodorkovsky's worth increased to an estimated 15 billion.

So the "business model" of this curious "wolf" can very simply be described as the way to earn rapidly billions of dollars with a minimum of work, but with good political connections.

Another tycoon who has more or less adopted this model is Chinese Ye Jimming who has succeeded to create in communist China the private conglomerate CEFC with assets in China and several foreign countries, including oil and gas, banks, real estate, medias etc.

Under a different chapter, one can find Marc Rich described by Tahereh Amirzadeh as "The fugitive who invented the spot market".

His major and crucial contribution was to understand and to put in practice the necessity to introduce flexibility in international oil and gas trade, through completing rigid and long-term contracts by immediate and short-term deals.

Marc Rich has been able to achieve this breakthrough by playing the role of a private and discreet middleman, known for using bribes as lubricant to facilitate business in relations with countries under sanctions or considered as enemies.

Last but not least a striking modern representative of the "oil wolves" is Charif Souki, a Lebanese who came to the USA as a student and stayed there because the civil war in Lebanon. With no diploma, no capital and no connection whatsoever with oil ang gas, he decided to become an entrepreneur, first as an investment banker and later on in oil and gas exploration and finally as a key actor in the completely unexpected boom of the shale gas in the United States over the last 10-20 years. His major challenge and achievement was the construction of a large terminal which was initially intended to import and regasify liquefied natural gas (LNG) to be imported from Algeria and other gas exporting countries. Souki's company Cheniere Energy had raised billions of dollars to fund this project when the gas market was suddenly turned upside down by the shale revolution, starting in 2009-2010, with a national production booming at a rate nobody could foresee.

The consequence was that instead of being a country needing to import natural gas, the USA became not only self-sufficient but in a position to export more and more huge volume of shale oil and gas. A reversal which was a big blow to Souki's dream and several billion importing terminal, the collapse of Cheniere stocks and the prospect of bankruptcy. Facing this misfortune, the "wolf" decided to take advantage of this challenge by deciding to raise new funds in order to transform the import terminal scheme into an export shale gas terminal.

Despite his success, he was hit by another setback when one of his close partners, the famous raider Carl Icahn, organized a "putsch" against him, and obliged Souki to leave his responsibilities in Cheniere Energy that he uses to consider as his "baby". But once more, and with the same courage and perseverance he bounced back by co-founding in 2016 another company, Tellurian, that launched a major liquefaction and export facility at Driftport on the U.S.Gulf with a proposed capacity of 27.6 million tons per year. In June 2020, Souki was elected as Chairman of this major player on the U.S. shale market. So the business model of Charif Souki could be summarized in few words: Anticipate and act with determination whatever the difficulties and challenges.

Nicolas Sarkis

Nicolas Sarkis is a Franco-Lebanese economist specialized in the Oil & Gas industries.

Dr. Sarkis holds a bachelor of law from Beirut's Université Saint Joseph (USJ) in 1956 and a PhD in economics from Paris's Université Panthéon-Sorbonne in 1961. His university studies were completed by a banking specialization at Deutsche Bank in Germany in 1962-1963.

He established in 1965 and managed until 2012, in Beirut then in Paris, the Arab Petroleum Research Center (APRC), an independent organization for studies and publications on the oil and gas industry covering the Middle East, North Africa, Sub-Saharan Africa and the Caspian Sea region. Thanks to its long-established direct contacts with the main decision-makers in the national and international oil companies based in the leading oil and gas exporting countries, APRC provided subscribers to its five publications with independent and authoritative information they needed regularly, a thorough analysis of events in the oil and gas sectors and an assessment of economic and political events. APRC added value by outlining the background and interpreting what fresh news mean for the development of the oil and gas industries in the above-mentioned countries.

APRC's publications featured interviews with top officials from oil and gas companies and international energy organizations, in-depth analytical studies, papers and articles by leading experts on various aspects of the oil, gas and petrochemical industries, detailed statistics and first-hand information on contracts, projects and tenders.

Dr. Sarkis worked at the same time as Senior Adviser for several countries (Algeria, Iraq, United Arab Emirates, Angola, Congo-Brazzaville, Japan, etc.) and different international oil companies. He was one of the first experts to have recommended the nationalization of the hydrocarbon industry in Arab countries.

Dr. Sarkis published dozens of articles in International media as well as the following books:

- Le Pétrole, facteur d'intégration et de développement dans les pays arabes, 1962, Librairie Générale de Droit et de Jurisprudence (LGDJ), Paris (translated into Arabic) ;

- Le Pétrole et ses incidences sur l'économie du Moyen-Orient, Beirut, 1965 ;

- The petroleum problem in Lebanon (in Arabic), Beirut, 1972 ;

- Le Pétrole à l'heure arabe, Stock, Paris, 1975 (translated into Arabic and Farsi) ;

- Oil & Gas in Lebanon: Blessing or Curse?, Beirut, 2015.

At the same time of his activities as Chairman of APRC, Dr. Sarkis organized in Paris, in association with the Franco-Arabic Chamber of Commerce, ten seminars on Oil & Gas Relations between France and Arab countries.

He also established in 2010 Solarmed who organized in 2011, in the "Palais des Congrès" of Paris, the first International conference / exhibition on the development of solar energy in the Mediterranean countries.

Since 2012, he has been writing several articles in the Lebanese press about the oil & gas resources in offshore Lebanon and the direct and indirect influence of several Lebanese politically exposed persons (PEPs), political parties and corrupt civil servants on the country's oil and gas policy.

1. Rockefeller, the creator of the vertical integration in the oil industry

In the oil & gas industry, there are mainly three business divisions: upstream (exploration & production) which includes the identification of deposits (discovery), the drilling of wells and the recovery of raw materials from underground (onshore or offshore); midstream which links upstream and downstream operations as it includes storage and transportation such as pipeline; and, downstream which includes oil refineries, petroleum product and natural gas distributors, petrochemical (including methanol, ammonia and urea) and liquefied natural gas plants and retail outlets (service stations).

The Rockefeller family is originally from France. Like many French protestant families, they moved to the US because of the conflict between Catholics and Protestants.

John D. Rockefeller started his oil business venture in the upstream activity. Soon, however, he realized that in order to keep costs down and earn more profits, he should control the entire supply chain from upstream to downstream. He wanted to keep margins high in order to be more resilient during crisis.

His cost policy was based on economies of scale and economies of scope. He acquired woodlands for lumber to manufacture his own oil barrels. He also built kilns on-site to dry the lumber. This saved shipping weight on its way to his own cooperage. He reduced from 40 to 39 the number of drops of solder to close the lids of kerosene cans.

By controlling his own supply chain, Rockefeller edged out his competitors.

His business model was the vertical integration (oil production, refining, transportation and marketing) to protect his investment from market volatility, to face competition and to succeed on long run.

What we call today an international oil company (IOC) is actually a fully integrated oil & gas company.

With that business model, only five years after getting into the oil & gas business (late 1860s), Rockefeller's company had the world largest oil refining capacity.

To support his model, he maintained high liquidity (strong cash position) and margins (keep costs down). This strategy allowed him to take advantage of crisis to acquire strategic assets and companies but also to upgrade his plants and improve quality while controlling costs.

At the end of the 1860s, he owned the world largest refinery. In 1870, he created Standard Oil Company, one of the world's first and largest multinational. His success story had just started.

The 1870s were years of crisis: overproduction, storage tanks overflows and fall of the oil price. There were too many producers, oilfields and refineries.

Rockefeller launched a battle. His plan was to friendly and peacefully buy out the leading refiners and dominant firms. Whenever he couldn't, he started a war against his competitor: he cut prices in the local market to force him to operate at a loss and then to beg Standard Oil for a takeover. By 1879, Standard Oil controlled 90% of US refining capacity. Rockefeller won.

Standard Oil also controlled most of the pipeline network in the US because transporting oil via pipeline was cost efficient and for Rockefeller it was a way to control the crude oil price processed into his refineries. His network was constituted of several small pipelines.

In 1879, the competitors of Rockefeller successfully built the world's first long distance oil pipeline, the Tidewater Pipeline (110 miles, i.e. 177 km). Long-distance pipelines were used by Rockefeller's competitors to compete with railroads because Standard Oil controlled railroad (bulk) shipments and then the oil & gas industry. They thought it could be an alternative transport system that could change the power balance.

Rockefeller was surprised by that major technological achievement (at that time) but did not see it as threat but rather as a proven technology in which he could invest in from now on. Indeed, he moved himself in the building of four similar pipeline. He even became a minority shareholder of the Tidewater Pipeline (in 1881). By 1885, three-quarters of oil was transported by pipeline rather than on rails. The competitors of Rockefeller were defeated. All together they had less than 20% of the oil industry.

Their last tool was to attack Rockefeller's monopoly politically and legally in courts.

At that time, Standard Oil's empire included 25% of all the US domestic oil wells, 4,000 miles of pipeline, 5,000 tank cars, 80% to 90% of the world oil refining capacity and of the US pipelines[1]. Standard Oil had over 100,000 employees[2].

Rockefeller was the richest man in the world, even richer than the biggest US bank.

Standard Oil was accused of breaching the US antitrust law and was then forced to dismantle:

---

[1] Steven K. Scott, *Mentored by a Millionaire: Master Strategies of Super Achievers*, John Wiley & Sons, 2010.

[2] John P. Hunter III, *Money for Power*, John P. Hunter III, 2014.

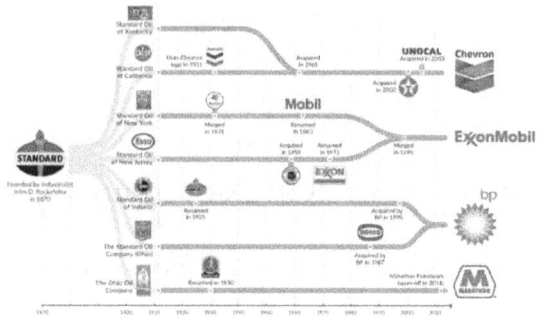

Chevron, ExxonMobil (including Esso), BP (British Petroleum) and Marathon Petroleum are among the major IOCs.

During the end of the 1990s, Microsoft was also accused of breaching the US antitrust law by holding a monopoly power with its Personal Computer (PC) operating system (Windows): Microsoft released Internet Explorer versions (its internet browser) for Windows (its PC operating system) and put restrictions to uninstall it and to use other programs such as Netscape's Navigator which at that time controlled the market of internet browser. Most of the PC manufacturers (OEMs) were making PCs with Windows and then most of the consumers had a PC with Windows. In the early 2000s, a legal settlement was reached and Microsoft removed these restrictions.

Today, more and more voices call to apply the US antitrust law against Google, Apple, Facebook and Amazon (the "GAFA") but also Netflix, Airbnb, Nvidia/Tesla and Uber (the "NATU") as well as LinkedIn, Twitter, Yahoo and IBM. These US companies are facing competition from South-Korean (Samsung) and Chinese (Baidu, Alibaba, Tencent and Xiaomi, the "BATX") companies which use same practices.

If US antitrust laws were applied by French courts, Kering, Hermès, L'Oréal and LVMH (the "KHOL"), the French luxury groups which own brands such as Gucci, Dior, Guerlain, Louis Vuitton, L'Oréal, Garnier, Maybelline and Tiffany & Co could have some problems…

2. D'Arcy, the pioneer of the modern oil industry in the Middle East

Antoine Kitabgi Khan, Persia's commissioner-general at the Paris Exposition of 1900, originally from Caucasus (Armenia or Georgia), wanted to attract a British investor to invest for an oil concession in western and southwestern Persia. He was very close to Amin al-Sultan, Persia's Prime minister The British investors were not excited about Persia following the absence of oil discovery in the framework of Reuter's concession, the cancellation of the tobacco concession, the failure of the Persian Bank Mining Rights Corporation and the scandal over the national lottery swindle[3]. D'Arcy, an investor, speculator and dealmaker, was the only one to show interest.

In 1901, William Knox D'Arcy obtained from the absolute Persian monarchy a 60-year exclusive concession covering ¾ of the country (excluding the five northern provinces in order to avoid offending Russia which wanted to build a pipeline from Baku to the Persian Gulf but was eventually blocked by the British lobby in Persia) to search for and obtain, exploit, develop,

---

[3] Denis Wright, *The Persians Amongst the English: Episodes in Anglo-Persian History*, London: I. B. Tauris and Company, 1985.

render suitable for trade, carry away and sell natural gas, petroleum, asphalt and ozokerite. Under this contract, exports and imports were free from taxes and duties. D'Arcy never visited Persia. Neither during the negotiations nor during the operations. He used representatives.

D'Arcy's business model was then purely speculative but relied on a bet: investing in Persia, a country where so many foreign investments failed, to discover oil there while there was still no commercial producing well yet in the country.

For being granted this concession, D'Arcy bribed the three unexperienced Persians who were negotiating with him. D'Arcy was to own whatever oil he found in the country and pay the monarchy just 16% of any profits he would make without letting it to review his accounting. The concession contract favored him in terms of area size, duration and profit sharing.

At that time, the Persian monarchy was in economic decline: the government budget was in deficit and was then generating debts which resulted in mortgaging the country's natural resources while Britain and Russia were bribing the political decision makers.

From 1905, following the financial difficulties of D'Arcy because no oil had been discovered, the exploration work was financed by Burmah Oil Company. Before agreeing with Burmah Oil Company, D'Arcy negotiated with the French branch of the Rothschild family to sell his concession[4]. The British Government was worried about D'Arcy selling to foreign interests including to Russians.

Indeed, D'Arcy's efforts to discover oil were a drain on his fortune. He had to find a partner with strong financial bones. He wanted to remain involved in the business venture

---

[4] Denis Wright, *The English amongst the Persians during the Qajar Period 1787-1921*, London: Heinemann, 1977.

because he was sure to find oil if he was able to continue: his risk and his perseverance will pay!

The British Government feared that the sale of (part of) the concession to the French or the Russians would make them to lose influence in Persia in favor of these two rival powerful nations.

This is why the British Government decided to intervene and to find a British partner for D'Arcy. For that, they used Sidney Reilly, the "ace of spies", the "James Bond" of the "real life", a British spy who disguised himself as a priest collecting donations and convinced D'Arcy to partner with a British &

Christian company, Burmah Oil, in the "Concession Syndicate", later renamed the "Anglo-Persian Oil Company"[5]. Reilly wanted D'Arcy to choose his country (UK) rather than its rival (Russia) and his religion (Christianism) rather other's (Rothschild are Jews) but he also offered him a better commercial deal.

In 1908, oil was discovered. D'Arcy was right. He finally made a discovery which marked a turning point in the history of the oil industry and of the Middle East. Following that discovery, a pipeline was built

---

[5] Daniel Yergin, *The Prize: The Epic Quest for Oil, Money & Power*, Free Press, 2008, p. 125-126.

from the oil wells to the Persian Gulf and the world's largest refinery was constructed at Abadan[6]. Distribution depots were also established.

The Anglo-Persian Oil Company (APOC) – which later became Anglo-Iranian Oil Company (AIOC) – was then incorporated in 1909 and took over the ownership of the concession. It was then a subsidiary of Burmah (it then changed).

In 1914, the British Government decided to use fuel oil instead of coal for its Navy.

---

[6] Edith T. Penrose, *The Large International Firm in Developing Countries: The International Petroleum Industry*, Cambridge: The M.I.T. Press, 1968.

Following that decision, the British Government acquired a 51 per cent stake (and then up to 66 per cent stake) in the company which it will only sell on the stock exchange in 1987. It reimbursed D'Arcy for all his previous expenditures and granted him free carry interest (shares). He also remained director till his death in 1917.

The company, which became British Petroleum (BP) in 1954 following the nationalization by Iran's Prime minister Mohammad Massadegh of the Iranian Oil industry in 1951 (in order to develop his country rather than enrich the UK), was an arm of the British imperial strategic policy. It was vital for UK's economy: in addition to the Royal Navy and to factories and plants through UK, British cars, trucks and buses were run on cheap Persian oil.

Without Darcy's concession, the UK could not have reached oil independence for the Royal Navy during the World War 1[7].

---

[7] Margaret Carnegie, *William Knox D'Arcy: Australian Gold and Persian Oil*, Melbourne: Kildrummie Press, 1992.

3. Marc Rich, the fugitive who invented the spot market

In 1974, Marc Rich (born Marcell David Reich), who grew up in the US but was born to Jewish parents in Belgium, founded "Marc Rich + Co.", a Swiss-based private commodity trading company. He was very successful till 1992 when he failed to corner and manipulate the global zinc market in 1992 after investing $1 billion without hedging. Following management buyout in 1993 (Rich sold his 51 percent stake to the management of Marc Rich + Co), the company was renamed Glencore and merged with Xtrata to create Glencore Xstrata which became a public company listed on various stock exchanges.

Rich dropped his studies and joined Philipp Brothers, at that time the world's largest raw-materials and metals trading house. He became a trader.

In 1967, he invented the spot oil market (built on leverage, depreciation and cash flow) which made him rich and changed the world economy. His mind was fast and his strategy was aggressive. He could identify trends and seize any opportunity before anyone else and he was ready to go where nobody wanted to go (because of wars, coups or natural disasters) and to deal with people and countries nobody wanted to deal with. He anticipated the Arab oil-export embargo in 1973 by buying up crude oil before the price hike and sold on demand when it enacted. His spot market idea increased crude price from $2 per barrel to $140 per barrel in 2008. Instead of long-term sales & purchase agreements tied up and preferred by the majors (the "Seven Sisters", the big integrated oil companies), he started to execute one-off trades through a thick layer of shell and offshore front companies on papers and fixers, middlemen and business partners on the ground as well as bribes. He was buying and selling crude cargoes for immediate delivery like any other commodity. He persuaded the oil producing countries to refrain giving their oil to majors and instead selling straight to customers using him and keeping more revenues. With Rich handling financing, insurance, customs clearance, transport, shipping and storage, most of these producing countries which were poor and unstable could become reliable exporters for all the customers. With his business model, he could make profits when the Arab started the oil embargo while the majors were struggling. He could even bypass the Arab oil embargo by supplying oil to US customers. Rich left Philipp Brothers because his boss refused to pay him a bonus.

Although his success is mainly due to his talent, Rich is also known for bribing the decision makers in these oil producing countries such as Nigeria. That was his way to enter business in these countries, do business with them and maintain business with them. Till the Foreign Corrupt Practices Act in 1977, the US were allowing their citizens to bribe foreign officials.

Marc Rich did a weapons-for-oil swap to Ecuador[8]. He was the first to do large commodity swaps: in the 1980s, he brokered uranium-for-oil deals between South-Africa,

---

[8] A. Craig Coptas, *Metals Mean: How Marc Rich Defrauded the Country, Evaded the Law, and Became the World's Most Sought-After Corporate Criminal,* New York: Putnam, 1985.

Iran and the USSR. Indeed, he dealt with the Soviet Union but also with countries under sanctions such as Khomeini's Iran, Gaddafi's Libya, Castro's Cuba, Nicaragua of Sandinistas, Pinochet's Chile, Marxist Angola, Ceausescu's Romania, etc. He told his life in the book of Daniel Ammann ("The King of Oil: The Secret Lives of Marc Rich", St. Martin's Press, 2009). He claimed that he earned over $2 billion from delivering 400 million barrels of oil to South Africa from 1979 to 1993. Between 1979 and 1994, he traded between 60 million and 75 million barrels of Iranian oil per year. He was buying oil from Iran and handling both shipping and marketing (resale) since the Iranians couldn't do it themselves because of the sanctions. He called it a "service charge". Rich even sold Iranian oil to Israel. He was Israel's main supplier: 7 million to 15 million barrels a year. The bulk of the crude he provided to Israel was Iranian. Iran did not care suppling oil to its enemies. Being under sanctions, they just wanted to sell their oil. Rich offered them solutions.

He was at the same time a fugitive for the US courts and FBI (he was charged of income tax evasion of $48 million and dealing with an enemy state, Iran) since he fled the US in 1983 (till he was granted a controversial pardon in 2001 by US President Bill Clinton on the last day of his second presidential term) and an informant for the State Department (US) and the Mossad (Israel's intelligence service). He became Israeli, Spanish and Bolivian. Due to indictment, he was forced to sell his stake in 20th Century Fox to Rupert Murdoch in 1984.

He fled from the US to Switzerland and turned the country into a global oil trade hub where trademarks are not more important than personal relationships. He enriched Switzerland and all the banks operating within the Helvetic Confederation. Switzerland is today the home of Glencore but also Vitol, Gunvor and Mercuria plus

Trafigura (founded by Claude Dauphine who worked with Marc Rich).

4. Khodorkovsky, the oligarch who originated the modern Russian oil power

Mikhail Khodorkovsky is the son of a Jewish father and a Christian mother who were both chemical engineers. He also did Chemical studies.

During that time, he was an active member of the USSR's Communist Party and its youth.

Under the Perestroika program of USSR President Mikhail Gorbachev, entrepreneurship and economic liberalization were encouraged.

In 1987, with six partners, Khodorkovsky launched a company named Menatep trading in foreign currency and commodities. In 1989, he registered it as a bank, one of the first privately owned-bank in post-Soviet Russia.

He acquired assets formerly owned by the State. The most important one is his acquisition of Yukos (78% for $309 million), Russia's second largest oil company, through privatization auction (although he didn't offer the highest bid). Two years later, Yukos was listed on the stock market with a value of $9 billion with $45 billion assets.

Khodorkovsky became a tycoon and the richest man in Russia (the 16th richest man in the world). In 2003, his worth was $15 billion.

Critics started when the ruble was devalued in 1998 because Menatep collapsed like many of Russia's private banks and he diverted the good assets into one of his other banks at the expense of the creditors.

Like the other Russian oligarchs, he benefited from Boris Yeltsin, the President of the Russian Federation. His problems started when Yeltsin resigned and Vladimir Putin, the new President, decided not allowing any interference of the oligarchs into politics.

Indeed, he funded opposition to Putin and lobbied legislation in favor of Yukos.

With a production of 1.7 million barrels of oil a day, Yukos was producing 20% of Russian oil, i.e. 2% of world's oil.

In 2003, he announced his plan to acquire Sibneft in order to make Yukos the fourth world largest oil producers and Russia's largest company.

He was then arrested and imprisoned on charges of fraud and tax evasion and then maintained in jail on additional charges of embezzlement and money laundering. He was released in December 2013 following his pardon by Putin in the framework of a larger amnesty in advance of the Winter Olympic Games (Sochi 2014). He immediately left Russia.

When ruling Yukos, Khodorkovsky wanted to attract foreign investments to Russia by showing transparency of oil data to the public. The oil business expanded in Russia aggressively, sometimes by barging Western companies out of the way in a style that would have been unacceptable outside of the Russian Federation. But Khodorkovsky soon realized the way to take on the biggest global players such as BP and Exxon was to attract foreign investment, and he did so by introducing unprecedented transparency to the Yukos accounts.

After his arrest the Yukos group was broken up and sold off, with many of its oil fields ending up in the hands of its smaller rival, now the giant Rosneft.

The British group BP and Qatar now own each almost 20% of Rosneft, while Khodorkovsky's lawyers and former Yukos shareholders continue to challenge the original transfer of Yukos assets in court.

Some say that the real reason of Khodorkovsky's arrest was that he was a key part of a Western intelligence operation against Russian's interests. It is true that

Khodorkovsky set up Open Russian Foundation (imitating Open Society of US billionaire George Soros) and invited Henry Kissinger and Jacob Rothschild and was himself named to the Advisory Board of Carlyle Group along with George H. Bush and James Baker. It is also true that before his arrest, he transferred 40% of Yukos to Jacob Rothschild.

5. Souki, the untired business model inventor & reinventor

Charif Souki is an American businessman and entrepreneur, born in Cairo, Egypt within a Lebanese Christian Greek-Orthodox family who moved to Lebanon, fleeing the United Arab Republic of Abdel Nasser. He never did any geology or engineering course. He started as a sales investment banker on Wall Street with Blyth, Eastman Dillon & Co. After an experience in restoration, he specialized in providing finance for small capitalization oil & gas companies.

In 2013, he was the highest-paid CEO of all U.S.-based publicly traded companies (he earned $142 million that year). The reason

was he earned $133 million in stock awards.
From August 2008 to December 2013, shares
in Cheniere Energy were up nearly 1,800%.

Share price between August 2008 and
December 2013:

Charif Souki is a co-founder and former chairman of the board of directors, chief executive officer and president (from September 1997 to December 2015) of Cheniere Energy.

In order to get fast access to stock exchange and investors, Charif Souki took over a listed shell Hollywood film-colorization company and renamed it "Cheniere Energy", publicly traded since July 3, 1996 under this name. He wanted his company to be in the stock exchange fast. This is why he acquired a shell company (with almost no asset) which was already listed on the NASDAQ and then raise equity and debts to finance his business model (which eventually changed three times, including two major failures).

The initial business model of Cheniere was oil & gas exploration & production. For that, Cheniere got involved with a proprietary 3-D seismic exploration program in the transition zone of Cameron Parish, southern Louisiana by acquiring 50% working interest participation in the framework of an Exploration Agreement with Zydeco. Non-operator in that prospect, Cheniere intended to be an operator for other oil & gas exploration prospects. Cheniere engaged geophysicists as consultants and then as employees.

Then, Cheniere acquired 3-D seismic data and dip move out (DMO) data in the shallow waters offshore Louisiana and Texas. Because Cheniere did not own drilling equipment, independent contracts were conducting the drilling operations.

Cheniere's drilling prospects and operations were not successful and were becoming expensive. For this reason, Charif Souki concluded that the United States held not enough natural gas. For him, the discussion about shale gas reserves was not relevant. He did not believe that they could be produced.

In 1999-2000, Charif Souki reinvented Cheniere's Business Model by turning the company's focus on the development of a liquefied natural gas (LNG) receiving terminal. His new idea was to import gas from major producing countries such as Algeria, Australia, Qatar and Russia, looking for new off-takers, to the United States. The challenge was that in order to be shipped, natural gas has to be turned into a liquefied form through a refrigeration process which reduces natural gas to a small part of its volume. Once arrived at its destination, the liquefied natural gas (LNG) has to be regasified, i.e. to be processed to return it to a gaseous state and deliver it to pipeline.

In 2001, Cheniere hired LNG experts and acquired options to enter into long-term leases for terminal sites in the Texas and Louisiana Gulf Coast. Texas and Louisiana are the second and the third largest natural gas-consuming states in the U.S. Cheniere's model was then to build, own and operate (BOO) these LNG receiving and regastification terminals.

Cheniere submitted to FERC applications for permits to build these LNG receiving and regasification facilities and also for permit applications for the associated pipelines. Bechtel was selected to do the engineering, procurement and construction (EPC) for facilities and Black & Veatch Pritchard was selected for the front-end engineering design (FEED) studies.

At that time, the LNG market was small but a growing one. The LNG producers were, however, not considering the US as a market for them. Moreover, the US had only four old LNG importing and regasification terminals. The US oil & gas industry believed that the country had enough natural gas and then did not need to import LNG. Souki, however, did not share the same opinion and decided that Cheniere Energy should raise funds to set up a big LNG importing and regasification terminal. In addition, he would have to convince the US regulators to give to Cheniere Energy permission to set up the terminal and the LNG producers to supply to the US (this is what he started to do from summer 2000) and to pay his company a fee for regasification in order to sell gas domestically instead of LNG which was not of interest to the US oil & gas industry. For that project, he needed to raise funds, which was initially a real challenge.

Finally, Cheniere Energy could spend billions in setting up this terminal but the US shale gas revolution in 2009-2010 hit hardly the company: the gas production doubled from 2008 to 2010, the US domestic gas price fall, the world demand raised and the shares of Cheniere Energy became traded for about $3. At that time, Cheniere Energy was facing two billion dollars of debt including one billion dollars due 2012 and was burning its annual $50 million revenue from arrangement with BG, Total and Chevron. In addition, Souki was facing exasperations from the board members and the investors. He was thinking on several plans.

Souki was offered by the Blackstone Group and Paulson & Co, two major investors in Cheniere Energy, to wipe out part of the debt against giving up control. He refused and planned to increase the debt of his company by raising cash, his expertise, to fund his new strategy: turning the LNG importing and regasification terminal into a gas purification and LNG exporting terminal.

Souki was convinced that his strategy of reconfiguring the terminal could be implemented. In 2010, he requested an estimate from Bechtel, a top engineering, procurement and construction (EPC) company. Bechtel estimated that it would cost $8 billion.

The new project would allow the shipment of 18 million tons of LNG per year. For that, Souki needed to raise a total of $12 to $16 billion new debt, including the financial costs and other expenses, two years only after the world financial crisis and while the financial markets were still recovering. Souki was, however, confident that he could obtain the permits and raise that amount because of his personal skills and experience and the fact that Cheniere Energy had an existing terminal.

His objective was for Cheniere Energy to be able to export two billion cubic feet a day, i.e. 3% of US domestic gas production.

The board of Cheniere Energy did not show much excitement but did not reject Souki's idea because there were not many alternative options to save the indebted company (with $18 billion once the new debts raised).

The challenge was that Cheniere Energy was a small company trying to compete with oil majors much better connected to the US regulators. Despite that, Cheniere Energy made an official announcement in June 2010 about its new intention. Although the Obama administration backed LNG exports, most of the oil & gas experts laughed at Souki. In 2011, Cheniere Energy started, however, the conversion works and less than two years after, Souki proved these experts wrong. He succeeded to raise funds and to increase Cheniere Energy stock value, which made him the most well-paid CEO of the listed companies on the US stock exchanges. Cheniere Energy is also now building a second terminal, which would increase the total investment of the company to about $30 billion. Souki's bet has then paid off for patient investors. Today, although his administration backs the coal industry, US President Donald Trump supports LNG exports by Cheniere Energy and wants to use the US LNG exports in his trade policy and in the US diplomacy. Indeed, Cheniere became the first company to export LNG from the US.

He left Cheniere Energy because of disagreement with Carl Icahn, a board member who has become the largest shareholder of the company. Souki believed that no dividends could be distributed to the shareholders before 2019 because of the cash flow while Icahn thought it could be done in 2016. In November 2018, Cheniere Energy reported a $65 million for the third quarter of the year and a net income of $404 million in the first nine months of the year. The company raised its distributable cash flow guidance to ranges between $0.5 billion to $0.6 billion in 2018 and $0.6 billion to $0.8 billion in 2019.

Share price between 7 January 1996 and 31

December 2015:

6. Ye Jianming, the shadowy oil baron of China's One Belt One Road initiative

Ye Jianming, a former Chinese mysterious tycoon, is the founder of CEFC China Energy, a private Chinese sprawling conglomerate including oil & gas assets and banks but also real estate, medias and sport in China and countries of Eastern Europe, Africa, former USSR and the Middle East. Initially, the company was an obscure niche fuel trader in Eastern China. It became an international energy giant doing deals in countries where there is war such as Chad, South Sudan and Iraq and with pariahs like

North Korea. Ye tried to be a middleman to remove sanctions against Iran.

From 2009 to 2018, CEFC's revenues jumped from $48 million to $44 billion but according to some reports they were inflated by fake trading in order to gain access to debt financing. By 2018, CEFC had a global property portfolio worth $3.2 billion and employed 50,000 people. CEFC was ranked No. 222 on the 2017 Fortune 500 list.

Rumors say that he was backed by the People's Liberation Army and even by Chinese President Xi Jinping (with whom he appeared with during a state visit to the Czech Republic) because of high-profile overseas acquisitions. According to Financial Times, CEFC was sponsoring a pro-China think tank with ties to retired military intelligence officers and was doing business with the military's 'princeling' elite[9]. His main creditor was China Development Bank (CDB), a Chinese State-owned bank investing in international projects. CDB provided two third of the CEFC's financing. In 2017, CEFC could sign a $9.1 billion deal for the acquisition of a 14.16 percent stake in Rosneft, the Russian State-owned oil company. Such deal served Beijing's objectives. And, CEFC was involved in the

---

[9] https://www.ft.com/content/e3f8cbd2-983f-11e7-a652-cde3f882dd7b.

"One Belt One Road Initiative", the strategic plan of Chinese leader Xi for a New Silk Road.

Ye claimed he initially acquired Xiamen-based company Huahang through an auction of assets illegally obtained by Lai Changxing (who fled to Vancouver in 1999 to avoid arrest by the Chinese authorities). This small piston plant supplied the People's Liberation Army (PLA). Rumors of his ties with the PLA come from that fact. This company, however, never belonged to Lai. Ye probably acquired it through privatization. According to its old presentations, CEFC was actually created through the privatization of a company of the Sinostar Group. He pretends that he initially raised funds from wealthy investors in Hong Kong and in the Fujian province. His strategy was to "look at geopolitics" and to operate in the breaches left open by CNPC/PetroChina, Sinopec and CNOOC, the three Chinese State-owned major companies, mainly in the countries where it is easier to do business in or with as a Chinese private oil company rather than as a Chinese SOE. He aligned CEFC with the objectives of the Chinese government and appeared as Chinese Government's unofficial energy envoy meeting Heads of States and Governments around the globe.

If the shareholding structure of CEFC was private, its organization was like those of Chinese SOEs (it had a Communist Party Committee, a Youth Committee, etc.) and like in the army (regimentation and promotion).

In 2016, Fortune Magazine ranked Ye Jianming number two in its "40 Under 40" list of the most influential young people in business (French President Emmanuel Macron was only ranked number four).

He could expand CEFC's business by bribing decision makers to win contracts and by borrowing more than what he could.

Although he is detained since 2018 for investigation into 'suspected economic crimes' which could be possible corruption charges for bribing a former Communist party chief in Gansu province, the real reason may be that he had transferred a lot of capital out of the country and that he had a risky financial behavior, i.e. being over-leveraged. After his arrest, the deal with Rosneft collapsed. Ye could not secure financing for that deal. CEFC has been dismantled. Other rumors said Ye Jianming is the grandson of Ye Jianying, a "hero" of China's Communist revolution led by Mao who told that "Marshal Ye" saved the Communist Party, the Red

Army and China's People Republic. Ye Jianming denied that rumor.

7. Hamm, the father of the shale boom

Harold Hamm was the 13th child of Oklahoma sharecroppers. He was not even 17 when he started working at the Potter Oil Company. He was pumping gas in a gas station. At age of 21, he founded his own company, Harold Hamm Tank Truck Service, after buying one single bobtail Ford truck (a water pump truck) to deliver drilling fluids and to service drilling rigs. He was hauling water to and from oilfields. At age of 26, he took out a loan to drill his first well.

His company, Shelly Dean Oil Co., was named after his two eldest daughters. Before his 30th anniversary, he was operating multiple producing wells across Oklahoma.

He gambled on the Bakken oilfield in North Dakota and Montana as well as in the Scoop oil basin in Oklahoma. He became a millionaire and then a billionaire.

In 1985, he acquired Petro-Lewis and more than 500 oil & gas wells. In 1990, Shelly Dean Oil Co. was renamed Continental Resources.

He pioneered horizontal drilling and hydraulic fracturing to unlock oil & gas. He had the vision to use them. This transformed the US oil industry. In 2003, he entered North Dakota's Bakken shale play, now one of the largest oilfields in the continental US and one of the most productive US oilfields. Bakken is the biggest US oil find since Alaska's Prudhoe Bay in 1968.

His company went public in 2007 but he still owns more than the 3/4 of it. He used the proceeds to acquire more land in the Bakken.

In 2012, Continental became one of the 10 largest US oil producers with a production of more than 330,000 barrels per day, much of it from North Dakota.

He lobbied in favor of lifting the ban on US oil exports in late 2015, a decision which affected the international oil market.

Shale offered energy independence to the US.

His success in shale drilling in the Bakken field led to a shale rush. Today, the US became the world largest oil producer along with Saudi Arabia and Russia. That's because of fracking and horizontal drilling. Fracking is now used in most of the states of the US for gas and oil extraction. Fracking's epicenter remains North Dakota where Hamm started to use it for extracting oil & gas.

While the major oil companies (such as ExxonMobil, Chevron, etc.) were not part of the initial shale boom, hydraulic fracturing is responsible for almost all the new oil & gas wells in the US.

www.ingramcontent.com/pod-product-compliance
Lightning Source LLC
Chambersburg PA
CBHW070406220526
45467CB00001B/492